SRI JOYDIP ASHRAM

SUBHADIP

BENGAL'S BHAKTI CULTURE AND LITERATURE

EDITED BY SRI JOYDIP

1/5/2024

শুভদীপ

বাংলার ভক্তি-সাহিত্য সংখ্যা ২০২৪

Subhadip Literary Journal (BBS Edition 2024)
Published by : **SRI JOYDIP ASHRAM**
ISBN Number : 978-81-966007-7-8

Contents

DEDICATION

To those Spirtual leaders whose tapas has brought Bengal's Bhakti movement building an unique devotional literature and culture in India

Published and Printed by

Sri Joydip Ashram Publishers

An unit of Sri Joydip Ashram Gyan Yoga Training and Research Centre

A Tax Exempted NGO and member of UN Global Compact

93 Itbhata Road , Burdwan -3

Phone/ Whatsapp – 9007295256

Email – editor.subhadip@gmail.com

http://www.srijoydipashram.org

Editorial Team

Sri Joydip (Editor)

Alan Tupicoff (Guest Editor)
Amit Ghosh (Guest Editor)
Sharboni Chakladar (Guest Editor **and Visual Designer)**
Pradipta Sengupta (Guest Editor)
Shiladitya Chakladar (Guest Editor **and Documentary Filmmaker)**

Contributing Authors

Sri Joydip
Swami Vishnuananda

Editorial

The esteemed literary organization Sri Joydip Ashram Publications– the publication arm of Sri Joydip Ashram Gyan Yoga Training and Research Centre, boasts an impressive 75% membership and volunteer base actively engaged in literary pursuits.

In our pursuit of literary excellence, we have consistently strived to uphold the highest values and standards of Indian Ancient Gyan Yoga Tradition. Around four thousand five hundred years ago with the advent of Bhagvad Gita, Bhagvatam and Sri Krishna as a new model of Bhakti marga emerged . This new path brough some transforming change in the Indian Ancient Gyan Yoga literature and culture. However, it was after four thousand years of this sweeping change the real impact was visible in the eastern part of India where we had the undivided Bengal . This transforming impact can only happen with the advent of Sri Sri Chaitanya Deva who aroused and displayed such power of devotion that it completely changes the Bengali culture , literature and everything which goes with the identity of Bengal. After three fifty year from then , there emerged another powerful jolt when the space of bhakti created by Chaitanya deb has started to fade away. It was with the advent of Sri Ramakrishna Bengal because a land known for it 's unique culture and literature of Bhakti around the world.

Sri Joydip Ashram as a key player in the literary realm, we have witnessed firsthand the positive impact of bhakti and devotional service on the growth and success of literary associations and writers which has helped to build a society where Bhakti is appreciated as an highest form of sadhana.

As the NGO leader of Sri Joydip Ashram Gyan Yoga Training and Research Centre **(An Income Tax exempted Organisation and also member of United Nations Global Compact)**, our organization is committed to fostering that literary appreciation and promoting cultural understanding of Bengal's unique Devotional culture. This edition aims to delve into the profound nuances of **Bengali devotional literature**, offering a platform for scholars, writers, and enthusiasts to engage in meaningful discussions.

As an editor of this edition I expect this will host an **impactful journey** in, fostering a deeper connection with our **Bengal's rich Devotional literary heritage.**

The release of the **Subhadip Literary Journal** – Bengal Bhakti Literature and Culture edition is a significant aspect of this initiative, serving as a lasting documentation of the course of development of Bengal's Bhakti movement. This publication has featured **scholarly articles, creative works, and critical analyses, contributing to the broader discourse on Bengali devotional literature**.

I am also ambitious that this edition will enhance the visibility of our literary endeavors on for preservation of Unique Bengal's Devotional Culture heritage in International stage.

This is an ideal journal **which should be supported by the Government and institutional bodies of different scale**.

We believe that by supporting this initiative, you as a reader also are contributing to the preservation and promotion of our **Bengal's Devotional cultural heritage** to preserve the **rich literary heritage of Bengal's Devotional Culture**.

Sri Joydip

Sri Joydip

Editor

Subhadip Literary Journal

Swami Vivekananda and Literature of Parabhakti
by Sri Joydip

When this (Para bhakti) highest ideal of love is reached, philosophy is thrown away; who will then care for it? Freedom, Salvation, Nirvâna — all are thrown away; who cares to become free while in the enjoyment of divine love? "Lord, I do not want wealth, nor friends, nor beauty, nor learning, nor even freedom; let me be born again and again, and be Thou ever my Love. Be Thou ever and ever my Love." "Who cares to become sugar?" says the Bhakta, "I want to taste sugar." Who will then desire to become free and one with God? "I may know that I am He; yet will I take myself away from Him and become different, so that I may enjoy the Beloved." That is what the Bhakta says. Love for love's sake is his highest enjoyment.

SWAMI VIVEKANANDA

How does the detachment, of a Devotee arises ?

How does he grows, towards love or devotion ?

It can arrive from a very worldly plane or from a very worldly love.

A love can create , a love can destroy.

Even the very forms of worldly love, which comes in different love affairs , have both ability to create peace and prosperity , at the same time, have the ability to destroy and ruin the both of lives , to compel each other to suicide , to destroy relationships.

So every love has a quality of devotion in it.

Why do we get attracted, towards different things in the Universe ? Why do we get attracted, to different beings in the Universe ?

Is it just because of Outer shell , Outer nature , Outer beauty ?

Without consciousness no beauty has an attraction .

The root of our attraction is a divine consciousness, which gets expressed in different objects and different beings.

We are not really getting attracted to that object or being , but we are actually getting attracted to the divine, which is staying in a dormant , in a hidden way to that particular object.

Our most worldly love have traces of devotion.

What we need to do is, to find out the trace of devotion , find out the deeper connection , then only each love of world , each worldly love , can reach in the stage of its fulfilment , otherwise it can create a certain nervous excitement , but it cannot create the permanent joy – the Bliss , Wisdom and Completeness.

To create that completeness of love , you need to understand the principles of Bhakti Yoga. Bhakti Yoga is actually a transforming love , which transforms most ugliest form of love , into most highest form of love.

The love that destroys , the love that constantly creates pain , the love that is unethical , the love that makes us loss everything , can be also converted to the love which is healing, to the love which is complete , to the love which constantly gives us joy, by the principles of Bhakti Yoga.

When we see the ideal of the highest principle , when we see the working of divine, on each of the object in Universe, and each of the beings of Universe , and we make a point, of loving that object , of loving that being , not because of that object , not because of that person , but because that becoming an expression of the divine.

We see in everything thing around us , and every being around us, a presence of divine . And that makes all our love- pure, complete , fulfilled . It makes each love- divine . All the things we love, then starts giving fragrance of divine.How does the detachment, of a Devotee arises ?

How does he grows, towards love or devotion ?

It can arrive from a very worldly plane or from a very worldly love.

A love can create , a love can destroy.

Even the very forms of worldly love, which comes in different love affairs , have both ability to create peace and prosperity , at the same time, have the ability to destroy and ruin the both of lives , to compel each other to suicide , to destroy relationships.

So every love has a quality of devotion in it.

Why do we get attracted, towards different things in the Universe ? Why do we get attracted, to different beings in the Universe ?

Is it just because of Outer shell , Outer nature , Outer beauty ?

Without consciousness no beauty has an attraction .

The root of our attraction is a divine consciousness, which gets expressed in different objects and different beings.

We are not really getting attracted to that object or being , but we are actually getting attracted to the divine, which is staying in a dormant , in a hidden way to that particular object.

Our most worldly love have traces of devotion.

What we need to do is, to find out the trace of devotion , find out the deeper connection , then only each love of world , each worldly love , can reach in the stage of its fulfilment , otherwise it can create a certain nervous excitement , but it cannot create the permanent joy – the Bliss , Wisdom and Completeness.

To create that completeness of love , you need to understand the principles of Bhakti Yoga. Bhakti Yoga is actually a transforming love , which transforms most ugliest form of love , into most highest form of love.

The love that destroys , the love that constantly creates pain , the love that is unethical , the love that makes us loss everything , can be also converted to the love which is healing , to the love which is complete , to the love which constantly gives us joy, by the principles of Bhakti Yoga.

When we see the ideal of the highest principle , when we see the working of divine, on each of the object in Universe, and each of the beings of Universe , and we make a point, of loving that object , of loving that being , not because of that object , not because of that person , but because that becoming an expression of the divine.

We see in everything thing around us , and every being around us, a presence of divine . And that makes all our love- pure, complete , fulfilled . It makes each love- divine . All the things we love, then starts giving fragrance of divine.

Sri Aurobindo's Savitri: A Spiritual Odyssey and its Resonance with Bengal's Bhakti Tradition

By Special Correspondent

Introduction: Sri Aurobindo's magnum opus, "Savitri: A Legend and a Symbol," is a transcendent epic that delves into the realms of consciousness, spirituality, and the transformative power of divine love. While not directly rooted in the Bhakti tradition of Bengal, Savitri carries resonances that echo the core principles of Bhakti literature, bridging the gap between Vedantic philosophy and devotional practices.

Integration of Bhakti Elements: Though Sri Aurobindo's philosophy is primarily influenced by Vedanta and Yoga, Savitri incorporates elements that parallel the devotional ethos of Bengal's

Bhakti tradition. The poem explores the journey of the titular character, Savitri, as she seeks spiritual enlightenment and divine union. The theme of unwavering love, surrender, and the quest for the divine aligns with the Bhakti tradition's central tenets.

Divine Love and Surrender: In Savitri, the concept of divine love is portrayed through the relationship between Savitri and Satyavan. Their love transcends the mortal realm and becomes a symbol of the soul's yearning for union with the divine. This theme echoes the intense devotion found in the works of Bhakti poets like Chandidas and Jayadeva, who celebrated the soul's deep yearning for union with the Supreme.

Example: In Book XI of Savitri, Savitri's encounter with the Divine Mother, who guides her through the cosmic mysteries, reflects the essence of surrender and divine guidance found in the devotional literature of Bengal. This encounter mirrors the devotional songs where devotees seek solace and guidance from their chosen deity.

Yogic Synthesis and Devotion: Sri Aurobindo's integral yoga philosophy, which seeks the synthesis of the spiritual and material aspects of life, resonates with the inclusive nature of Bhakti literature. While emphasizing self-realization, Sri Aurobindo acknowledges the importance of love, devotion, and surrender as integral components of the spiritual journey.

Example: The synthesis of yogic principles and devotion is evident in Savitri's spiritual journey, where she not only engages in intense yogic practices but also surrenders herself completely to the divine will. This synthesis mirrors the holistic approach found in the Bhakti tradition, where practitioners combine meditation, prayer, and devotional singing to achieve spiritual awakening.

References:

Aurobindo, Sri. Savitri: A Legend and a Symbol.

Radhakrishnan, Sarvepalli. The Philosophy of Sri Aurobindo.

Das, Sisir Kumar. A History of Indian Literature: 1911-1956.

Conclusion: Sri Aurobindo's Savitri, though rooted in a different philosophical framework, shares profound resonances with Bengal's Bhakti tradition. The exploration of divine love, surrender, and the integration of yogic principles within the spiritual journey depicted in Savitri aligns with the core principles celebrated by the Bhakti poets of Bengal. The synthesis of Vedantic wisdom and devotional fervor in Savitri underscores the universal nature of spiritual truths, uniting diverse traditions on the common ground of seeking divine union.

Tips from Bhakti Literature of Bhagavad Gita by our Special Correspondent

How do a Bhakta or devotee turns every emotions into Godward emotions.

The deepest secret of Bhakti yoga is the renunciation which is practised in Bhakti Marga is much easier then Gyan Marga . In Bhagvad Gita , we find the comparision between Bhakti Yoga and Gyana Yoga . Krishna tells Arjuna that the path of Bhakti where a person surrender emotions ,and actions and knowledge, is much easier, then the path of Gyana as one has to detach from the world thinking it as a Maya in Gyana marga , where in Bhakti Marga detachment comes automatic with Surrender.

When we observe the deep experience of the Gopis . We see that the Gopies has the feeling of happiness and sadness on the reference point of Krishna . That destroys for them both the samskaras which originates from good karma and also destroys the samskaras which originates from bad karma.

As we know , the good samskaras are also obstacles in liberation like bad samskaras . So the Gopies in there love of Krishna destroys also the good samskaras , as feel happy when they have love of Krishna , and by that they removes all the samskaras created out of Good Karmas.The feeling of sadness comes from the period when they stay away from Krishna so even the bad karmas which creates samskaras are also removed due to these.

These way the Gopis attain the state of Parabhakti where both the good and Bad karamas are removed and they can be liberated with the power of spontaneous and continuous love for Krishna.

The Idea of Devotional Service in Devotional Literature

These are the three sutras on **Devotional Service from Chapter 9 [26,27,28] - The Yoga of Kingly Scienceand Kingly Secret**.

The 26th Verse tells about the minimum requirement of devotional service and how the percentage of Bhakti in your heart is important than the objects you are offering is clearly mentioned.

26th Verse : If one offers Me with love and devotion a leaf, a flower, a fruit or water, I will accept it.

In the 27th Verse Krishna gives wisdom on how every work can be turned into a offering . Mother of Pondicherry , gives a very short statement on these - **"Remember and Offer"** .

Karma Seva - While these stage doesn't happen to start with , one has to intially practise different forms of Seva - it can be "Karma Seva " - Doing different benevolent actions like giving education to the poor, and uneducated and then giving medical help to the needy . Sri Joydip Ashram have some projects on these line - and one can always start a new project in these lines . They can also associate it with the course assignment of our Bhakti Yoga Course, where having a seva project is also important .

Bhakti Seva - Then comes "Bhakti Seva" - you can shower your love to somebody without expecting anything for return . Some people really go to spend there time , with disabled children and make them feel good and these also make the children enjoy there presence and there love. There is an organisation often contacts us who looks after diabled children in Kolkata . If somebody wants to do something on these line they are welcome .

Gyan Seva - Then comes the "Gyan Seva " . These one thing Sri Joydip Ashram specializes . Gyana Seva which is aligned to our mission of Vidyavatra is the highest form of seva , and Sri Joydip Ashram teachers are specialized on these . We here spend a lot of time, educating people about scriptures and eternal spiritualprinciples. People are welcome to share there wisdom and Knowledge in there forum . Newbies can also introduce themselve and share there wisdom . These the way by sharing or Gyan Seva we can grow our understanding an Wisdom . In today morning only I recieved a requets from Gian of Brussels to join these forum . Filling up the part mentioning the reason of joining these forum and he talked about how he was following Sri Joydip Ashram Wisdom for a long time in web, and how he sometimes would understood things and sometimes could understand due to poor audio and also lack of clarity of Judgement . These forum would be a great oppurtunity for others like Gian, to also do Gyan Seva and create more wisdom with sharing . Once we have crossed these layers we can have a steady offering attitude inside your mind and we can offer everything what we work to divine.

27th Verse — Whatever you do, whatever you eat, whatever you offer or give away, and whatever austerities you perform – do that, O son of Kuntī, as an offering to Me.

These kind of attitude of steady offering which comes after performing Karma Seva , Bhakti Seva and Gyan Seva which is doing the three forms of Yoga - Karma - Bhakti- Gyana in the plane of service and seva we can attain these state , where no work would create bondage and we will be free from both auspicious and unauspicious results.

28th Verse — In this way you will be freed from bondage to work and its auspicious and inauspicious results. With your mind fixed on Me in this principle of renunciation, you will be liberated and come to Me.

Doing these three kinds of Seva , makes the mind purified and we start having more control over our mind and then it automatically gets fixed in an higher principle of renunciation . This makes them easy to get liberated and reach divine consciousness.

Chaitanya Charanmitra: Transformative Influence on Bhakti Literature and Tradition in Bengal by Swami Vishnunanda

Introduction: The Chaitanya tradition, rooted in the teachings of the 15th-century saint Chaitanya Mahaprabhu, has had a profound impact on Bhakti literature and the Bhakti tradition of Bengal. Among the notable facets of this tradition is the concept of Chaitanya Charanmitra, a term that encapsulates the transformative effect of Chaitanya Mahaprabhu's divine association on the lives of his followers.

Chaitanya Charanmitra and its Significance: Chaitanya Charanmitra, loosely translated as the 'nectar of association with Chaitanya,' refers to the spiritual companionship and influence that Chaitanya Mahaprabhu had on his devotees. This association played a pivotal role in shaping the devotional landscape of Bengal, leading to a rich and diverse body of Bhakti literature that expressed the intense love and devotion inspired by Chaitanya Mahaprabhu.

Effect on Bhakti Literature: The influence of Chaitanya Charanmitra is vividly reflected in the Bhakti literature of Bengal. Works such as the Chaitanya Bhagavata by Vrindavan Das Thakur and the Chaitanya Charitamrita by Krishnadas Kaviraj Goswami stand as monumental compositions that chronicle the life and teachings of Chaitanya Mahaprabhu. These texts not only serve as biographies but also capture the deep emotional and spiritual connection the authors felt through their association with the saint.

Chaitanya Charitamrita, for instance, describes the profound impact of Chaitanya Mahaprabhu on his followers, illustrating how their lives were transformed by his divine presence. The text cites specific instances where individuals underwent significant spiritual awakenings, showcasing the power of Chaitanya Charanmitra in fostering devotion.

Effect on Bhakti Tradition: Chaitanya Charanmitra played a crucial role in revitalizing the Bhakti tradition in Bengal, infusing it with fervor and ecstasy. Chaitanya Mahaprabhu's emphasis on the congregational chanting of the holy names, known as the 'sankirtan movement,' became a hallmark of the Bhakti tradition in the region. The tradition of ecstatic devotional singing and dancing, inspired by Chaitanya Mahaprabhu's teachings, continues to thrive in Bengal and has spread globally.

The Bhakti tradition of Bengal also witnessed the emergence of various devotional schools, such as the Gaudiya Vaishnavism, inspired by Chaitanya Mahaprabhu. Prominent Vaishnava saints like Narottama Das Thakur, Srinivas Acharya, and Syamananda Pandit further propagated the teachings of Chaitanya Mahaprabhu, contributing to the expansion and consolidation of the Bhakti tradition in Bengal.

Conclusion: Chaitanya Charanmitra, the nectar of association with Chaitanya, stands as a profound concept that encapsulates the transformative influence of the 15th-century saint on Bhakti literature and the Bhakti tradition of Bengal. Through the writings of devoted followers and the establishment of vibrant devotional communities, the legacy of Chaitanya Mahaprabhu continues to shape the spiritual landscape, inspiring countless individuals to embark on the path of divine love and devotion.

References:

Kaviraj Goswami, Krishnadas. Chaitanya Charitamrita.

Thakur, Vrindavan Das. Chaitanya Bhagavata.

Sardar, Marianne. "The Life and Teachings of Lord Chaitanya: An Introduction." The Bhaktivedanta Book Trust, 2005.

www.ingramcontent.com/pod-product-compliance
Lightning Source LLC
LaVergne TN
LVHW080819170826
845678LV00011B/2082

* 9 7 8 8 1 9 6 6 0 0 7 7 8 *